CW00480998

Can My Nuts Get Tangled?

And Other Embarrassing Questions Answered

Copyright © 2023 by Elwood Harrington

All rights reserved. No part of this publication may be reproduced, distributed, or transmitted in any form or by any means, including photocopying, recording, or other electronic or mechanical methods, without the prior written permission of the publisher, except in the case of brief quotations embodied in critical reviews and certain other noncommercial uses permitted by copyright law.

Disclaimer: The answers provided in this book are meant for entertainment purposes only. Please consult a qualified professional for serious inquiries. The author and publisher assume no responsibility for any unintended consequences resulting from the implementation of the answers provided herein.

Can my nuts get tangled?

Yes, your nuts can get tangled.

Imagine your nuts attempting a Tango dance routine, but they forgot to rehearse! They'll end up in a hilarious knot that even a top magician would struggle to untangle. It's like a comedy show in your pants!

It may sound funny, but for someone who have experienced this situation, it is anything but funny.

In a rare condition known as "testicular torsion", your balls may rotate around the spermatic cord and get tangled. The spermatic cord supplies blood to the balls. Hence, this rotation of your nuts can obstruct blood flow to your nuts. This can lead to swelling and severe pain.

The nuts don't usually twist on each other. Rather they twist on itself. It will feel better if you grab your ball and lift it. Because it takes the tension off of that twisted cord.

Testicular torsion requires immediate medical attention. If you feel sudden severe pain down there, seek medical attention right away.

Can I get a different penis through surgery if I don't like mine?

Yes and no.

Full penis transplant has been performed before. But the patients in those cases had some underlying conditions such as traumatic injury, botched circumcisions, removal of penis after surgery for penile cancer or severe micro-penis.

I mean two South African dudes who had this surgery lost their shafts during some taboo circumcision ritual. One American had penile cancer and his dick had to be removed. Another one had his dick and balls blown off by a bomb in Afghanistan. These people had a legitimate reason to undergo dick transplant.

Actually penis reattachment surgery dates back to 1970s. During that time, a Thai woman went berserk when she went on a dick-cutting spree on her ex-husbands and ex-lovers . Thai doctors performed at least 18 penis reattachments.

Dick replacement isn't done because you don't like yours. "I don't like my penis" is not an eligible criteria to have a dick replacement.

Did your manhood got snapped in half? Did a bomb blow off your woody? If not, why in God's name would you want a penis replacement surgery?

And even if you qualify for dick transplant, it is extremely hard to get a donor. Penis is not included as an organ that a DMV donor can donate.

They only option is to get the wang of a dead guy. Even that isn't easy to get by.

Dude, stop hating your dick. It's the only one you've got!

Can my dick explode from being too erect?

No, it won't. Your cock won't turn into a confetti cannon! While he might salute enthusiastically, there's no danger of him going all Michael Bay on you.

When you are extremely aroused, a lot of blood will flow into your private. It will become very hard. But it won't explode.

However, penile rupture might occur if an engorged penis bents suddenly during sexual activity.

Your trusty soldier knows when to stand at attention and when to stand down. And, there won't be any fireworks in the nether regions!

Why do people say that clitoris is hard to find?

To say in short... because it is tucked inside a woman's inner labia at the top of vulva under a protective hood.

Picture the clitoris as the VIP of the female anatomy, nestled in its own special nook. It's like the VIP room at a party – everyone's heard of it, but not everyone gets an invite!

Its location and feel is different from woman to woman, like a game of anatomical hide-and-seek.

You see, the clitoris isn't just a little nub; it's a multi-dimensional pleasure palace with hidden chambers beneath the surface. It's like trying to find your way around a fancy mansion – you might stumble upon a room you never knew existed!

Adding to the mystery, the clitoris doesn't have a neon sign pointing to it (like the boobs). It's a bit like trying to find Waldo in a sea of sensory information.

But fear not, intrepid explorers! With a little patience, communication, and perhaps a treasure map (or a handy anatomy lesson), discovering this hidden gem can be a delightful adventure for both parties involved.

And remember, practice makes perfect in this delightful quest for pleasure!

Is it normal to give off very long farts each lasting 30 seconds?

The world's longest recorded fart was 2 minutes and 42 seconds long.The name of this genius farter is Bernard Clemmens from London.

The length of a fart, my friend, is as diverse as the colors in a painter's palette. Just as no two artists create the same masterpiece, no two people produce identical gusts from their gastronomic gallery.

The average person farts about 14 times a day, and each fart can last from a fraction of a second to several seconds. The length of a fart depends on several factors, such as the amount and type of gas in the intestines, the pressure in the rectum, the tightness of the sphincter muscles, and the position of the body.

So, if you are giving off very long farts, it could be because you are eating or drinking something that makes you gassy, or you have a digestive disorder that affects your gas production or expulsion.

Or, it could be that you are just a talented farter who can control your sphincter muscles and release your gas in a prolonged manner.

Why do men have nipples?

Having nipples make more sense on women because they have the ability to breastfeed. But having nipples on males makes no sense, right?

Well, Mother Nature has a quirky sense of humor! In the early stages of development, before our bodies decide whether we will be male or female, we all start from the same basic blueprint. Nipples pop up before the gender-specific details get sorted out. So, men get to keep these quirky reminders of our shared origins. They are like the "just in case" feature, you might say.

Think of it this way. If men didn't have nipples, they would look like a different species from females. Females will be afraid to come near men.

So, kudos for male-nipples. They're like nature's little Easter eggs, giving everyone something to chuckle about!

Can I become allergic to another person?

Haven't we seen this kind of stuff in comedy movies and TV shows? But can it happen in real life?

The idea of developing an allergy to a fellow

human is like an unexpected plot twist in a sitcom! Rest assured, it's more of a Hollywood fantasy than a medical reality.

You see, allergies are typically triggered by substances like pollen, hair, clothing, sweat, semen, perfume, pet dander, or certain foods. Your immune system, in its wisdom, can sometimes get a bit overzealous and react to some harmless things as if they were major threats.

But becoming allergic to a person? Well, unless they've secretly transformed into a walking, talking pollen, it's highly unlikely. Our immune systems aren't wired to see humans as allergens. So, while you might develop a fondness allergy (commonly known as a crush), a true medical allergy to another person is about as probable as a unicorn showing up at your doorstep.

If you really feel like you are allergic to people, you might actually have a fear of being around other people. It is called "anthropophobia". You may need to see a psychiatrist for this.

All in all, allergic reactions to humans are safely confined to the realm of romantic comedies, not your everyday reality!

Why do sperm smell like bleach?

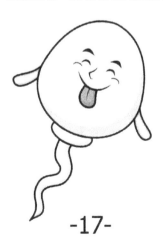

Now we arrive at the mystery of the peculiar scent of sperm, often compared to a household cleaner!

The aroma of sperm can be attributed to a compound called spermine. Spermine is like the rockstar of the reproductive system. It responsible for stabilizing DNA and keeping it in tip-top shape. But it also brings a distinctive fragrance to the party, one that some liken to the smell of bleach.

Think of it as Mother Nature's way of keeping things interesting in the bedroom. It's like saying, "Hey, I'm here to protect and serve... with a benign fragrance!"

Semen also contains ammonia, which is a common ingredient in household cleaning products. Sperm cells are made of proteins, so they naturally contain some ammonia. The seminal fluid that carries the sperm also has other alkaline substances, such as magnesium, calcium, zinc, and sulfur. All of these contribute to its distinct smell.

The bleach-like smell of semen is actually a sign of its health and fertility.
So remember, the scent of sperm is a quirky quirk, not a cause for concern. Embrace the oddities of biology and carry on with a chuckle!

Can shoving lemon or pouring Coca-Cola into vagina prevent pregnancy after unprotected sex?

Sounds silly but women have used these as contraceptive measures. Some women in the 18th century used to insert half a lemon into their lady bits. They believed that lemons kill sperms. Women in Moldova still uses this method.

Some women in 1960s used Coca-Cola to kill sperms in the vagina. They used to shake the bottle to build pressure and then blast it in their beaver. Their favorite one was "diet coke". Even today some women believe that Coke or other soda can kill sperms due to a sugar overdose.

Gals, don't even think of doing these. Lemon or Coke can irritate your vagina and cause infections. But if you live in Moldova, help yourself.

If I hold my poop longer, will my body absorb more nutrients from it?

Dude.. seriously?

Your digestive system is a team of diligent workers in the nutrient extraction factory. They're all lined up, ready to process the incoming goodies. Now, will holding onto your precious cargo for an extended period lead to a nutrient gold rush? Well, not quite.

You see, your body's nutrient-absorbing heroes, the small intestine cells, are highly efficient. They don't play favorites, and they certainly don't give extra credit for extended storage. They grab what they need, and they do it promptly, whether your poop has been marinating for hours or you're running on a tight schedule.

In fact, holding onto your poop for too long can actually lead to some rather unpleasant consequences. Your stool can become drier and harder, turning the exit strategy into a game of "Poop Plinko." Not exactly a fun-filled afternoon!

So, holding your poop longer is not a good idea at all. It will not make you healthier or smarter, but it will make you miserable and sick. The best thing to do is to listen to your body and go when you feel the urge. Your poop is not your friend, it is your enemy. Let it go, and you will be free.

If you want to help your body absorb more nutrients, chew your food properly. Don't eat too much food. Eat nutritious food. Drink plenty of water. Exercise regularly.

But if you really want your body to reabsorb more things from your stool, go ahead.

Hold your poop. But you will have stony poop. You'll need see a doctor who might use a stone-cutter to remove poop from your butt. And your butthole may need some suturing.

What does a human brain smell like?

You better ask those hillbilly from the movie "Wrong Turn". Because they are used to eating human brains.

Actually, human brains have no particular smell. Any odor comes from the structure surrounding the brain. For example: during a surgery, an open brain is surrounded by lots of blood. And the smell that you will have is that of the blood.

Does anyone regret marrying someone with a small penis?

Look, marriage is not all about dick size, tight vagina, porno-style hard sex, rectal rooters and so on. You'll care for your partner. You will spend your life together and create a family with your partner.

On the other hand, satisfying sexual desires and fantasies is an integral part of adult life. If a male partner has a micro penis, it can create a big problem indeed.

This is a topic as sensitive as a cat with a sunburn! First and foremost, let's get one thing straight: love is not measured in inches or centimeters. It doesn't come with a ruler, a measuring tape, or a scoreboard. Love is a grand symphony, a cosmic ballet, and it dances to its own tune.

To assume that the size of one's meat is the sole determinant of marital bliss is like believing that a chef's worth is determined by the size of their spatula. Nope. It's the culinary prowess, the finesse, the artistry that truly matters!

Now, if someone finds themselves fixated on the anatomical specifics, perhaps it's time for a recalibration of priorities. Love, respect, communication, and shared values – these are the cornerstones of a successful marriage, not the measurements of one particular appendage.

After all, it's not the size of the ship, but the motion of the ocean. In the vast sea of love, we're all setting sail together! Right?

But at the end, it really depends on the person. If they are fascinated about huge penis, they should not marry a person with small penis.

Why do I pee in two streams after an erection?

Actually this is not uncommon. If you peed normally before erection, then everything is fine. It will get back to normal after your excitement subsides.

Your body has a nifty little valve called the urethral sphincter. When you have an erection, this sphincter gets a bit agitated. As a result, when you go to relieve yourself, the first few drops of piss might split into two streams.

Also your piss-tube may be compressed due to excitement. This may cause pee to squirt sideways. It may also be caused by some leftover semen inside your dick.

But this is usually a passing phase. Your pee will likely return to its regular, well-behaved self once the excitement subsides. If you find this phenomenon persists or causes discomfort, reach out to a healthcare professional for a bit of expert guidance.

Even our bodily functions have a sense of humor, and it's perfectly okay to have a chuckle about it!

Is it true that peeing on your wound helps you heal it?

No.. no... no. Don't even think about it.

Urine is not sterile, even before it comes out of you. It is a waste material from your body. Urine can contain bacteria that can cause infections, especially if you have a urinary tract infection or a STD.

The best way to clean wound is pouring clean water, soap water or saline water on it. So, while peeing on a wound might be a quirky campfire story, please keep your golden showers in the bathroom, where they belong!

If you hold your fart too much, what happens?

That's a stupid-ass thing to do. It can cause discomfort, cramping, pain and bloating. Because if you hold your fart, most of the gas stays in your digestive system. Your body may absorb some of the gas.
If you do it excessively, you may start burping fart. Now you wouldn't want to do that, would you?

Does masturbation cause muscle imbalance?

So, will you develop a massive Popeye arm versus a smaller arm if you masturbate with one arm only? Not really. You must have seen such jokes on Facebook or Instagram. But that's just ridiculous.

You may develop some sort of imbalance in the long run. One arm may develop slightly better tone but it will be barely noticeable. So, you don't have to worry about it.

Poop gets stuck in my butt hair. What can I do?

Dingleberries, huh? While you wipe after taking a poop, you may feel some tiny granules hanging by a thread, or hair actually. You try to clean, but they remain stuck. Desperately you try to yank it out. You feel a brief pain. And you got a dingleberry in your hand.

Pinch and pull is the most common method to get rid of dingleberries. But it is painful and risky. Pulling out ass hair may cause infections down there.

A better way is to cut it out. Use a grooming tool to cut the hair. This will relief the pain of pulling at your booty hair. Another way is to soak it and wash it with soap & water.

If you decide to shave down there, take care not to cut yourself.

All these for those darn dingleberries!

If I hold and stop semen in the middle of ejaculation, will it go back into my balls?

Reverse flow of semen during ejaculation is not possible.Don't even try to do that. Trying to ejaculate and holding it in the middle to stop semen from coming out is a silly thing to do.

When you ejaculate, semen is pushed forward by muscle contractions. It is a one way traffic. The expelled semen cannot get back into the balls. It will make its way out.

Even if you try to hold, it will drip out eventually. It will come out when you pee next time or when you have a wet dream. Ha ha.

If I wank too much, will I run out of semen?

You may run low on semen, but you won't run of of sperms.

When a man ejaculates, he releases semen that contains up to 300 million sperms. Each testicle produces about 200 million sperms everyday! So, you will not run out of sperm. Masturbation does not affect the long-term production of sperm.

However, frequent masturbation and ejaculation does make your semen thin and watery. Because you are not giving your body enough time to produce the semen.

But why would you masturbate too much? I heard of a Chinese dude who masturbated 100 times on a day and ended up having a brain stroke. So, if you want something like that happening to you, help yourself! After all, it is your shaft I'm talking about. You own it. Use it in whatever way you like, man!

If, theoretically, all the water in a person's body turned into wine, what would happen?

That person will die within minutes. Wine is acidic with a pH level between 3 and 4. Blood has a pH of around 7.2.

If all the water of a human body turns into wine, it would kill the platelets. Oxygen won't get carried to the cells. All the chemical reactions will stop. All the normal processes will become imbalanced. The ion balance will be disrupted. There will be an increase of ethanol in blood. It will make the blood very toxic.

Let's do some math. Human body contains around 60% water. A 90 kg person contains 54 kg of water. Wine contains around 12% of alcohol. If all the water turns into wine, that person will have 6.5 kg of pure alcohol in their system.
The normal activity of the heart will stop. Multiple organ failure will occur.

That dude will be a dead meat walking!

Why can't humans grow back their limbs like a lizard or an axolotl?

May be it's not worth it.

The ability to regenerate something is much more developed in lower organisms suck as bacteria, fungi, plants, starfish etc.

You see, it's all about some special cells. Lizards and axolotls have these magical cells called pluripotent stem cells. They're like the superhero shape-shifters of the cell world. When the need arises, they can morph into whatever body part is required – a tail, a leg, you name it!

Meanwhile, mammals have more complex biological structures. Limb regeneration would require complex control to ensure that they don't grow out of control, like cancer. Hence, mammals have no limb regeneration capacity.

The cells in our body have specific jobs and are not so keen on changing careers. So, if you're hoping for a lizard-style limb revival, you might be in for a bit of disappointment.

Some human organs can regenerate. If a piece of liver is removed, it can regrow back. If we lose a part of skin, it can regenerate up to certain extent.

But hey, don't despair! We humans have plenty of other superpowers that lizards can only dream of. Like, say, rocket science and interpretive dance. So, while we may not have the regenerative prowess of our reptilian pals, we've got plenty of other tricks up our sleeves!

Can I have an orgasm without ejaculation?

That's called a dry orgasm and it happens. Dry orgasm is where excitement meets the world's driest party!

If you failed to ejaculate even after hitting the climax during sex or masturbation, you had a dry orgasm. You had a ejaculation but no semen came out of your dick.

This may be caused by nerve damage, surgery, radiation therapy, blocked sperm duct, low testosterone or lack of sperm.

If I eat lots of carrots, will I turn orange?

Does eating carrots make you concerned of becoming the next Oompa-Loompa sensation?

Well, it depends on how many carrots you eat and for how long. Carrots are rich in beta-carotene, a pigment that gives them their orange color and also contributes to your skin's natural glow. However, if you eat too many carrots, or other foods that contain a lot of beta-carotene, you may end up with a condition called carotenemia, which is a yellow-orange discoloration of the skin. This is not harmful, but it may not be very attractive either.

According to a nutritionist, you would need to eat about 20 to 50 milligrams of beta-carotene per day for a few weeks to raise your levels enough to see skin discoloration. One medium carrot has about 4 milligrams of beta-carotene in it. So, if you're eating 10 carrots a day for a few weeks, you could develop carotenemia.

However, if you're eating a balanced diet that includes a variety of fruits and vegetables, you're unlikely to turn orange from carrots.

So, while a carrot-a-day is undoubtedly a healthy choice, don't worry about waking up with a sudden craving for a carrot-themed Halloween costume. Your skin won't turn into a vegetable patch anytime soon.

Is cannibalism bad for health?

Before answering question, I would say that cannibalism is bad for your social life. Because you won't have any friends or family left if you just eat them!

Cannibalism is dangerous for health. Eating human flesh can expose you to a variety of diseases and parasites, such as kuru and prion diseases. These conditions can cause neurological damage, dementia, and even death. For example: if you eat your partner's brain, you could get a disease called "kuru". It is similar to mad cow disease. Your brain starts working abnormally, you start trembling and may eventually die.

So, trying to make a sandwich with yourself as the main ingredient – definitely not on the menu for maintaining good health! Try to imagine explaining your meal choices at a dinner party!

Let's leave the self-serving snacks to the realm of science fiction and horror movies. Your body and your social circle will thank you!

Does the body smell of a man attract woman?

The invisible love potion supposedly wafting from our pores! You must have heard about them... pheromones.

Pheromones, those sneaky little chemicals, are thought to play a role in attraction. It's like nature's way of giving us a secret weapon in the dating game.

You can picture pheromones as your wingman, whispering sweet nothings to the noses of potential admirers. They're like tiny, scent-based cupids, working behind the scenes to spark that special spark.

But here's the twist: pheromones don't come with a universal manual. What smells enticing to one person might be a fragrant faux pas to another.

So, while a dash of natural aroma might add a touch of allure, it's probably best not to rely solely on your body's fragrance for romantic success. A little cologne, a lot of charm, and a hefty dose of genuine personality will go a long way!

Can you get cancer from standing too close to a microwave?

No, you won't. Fear not, my microwave-wary friend!

Microwave ovens heat food by resonantly stimulating the water molecules in food and increasing the temperature of the food. But they don't ionize the atoms of what is being cooked. It uses non-ionizing radiation i.e. non-cancer-forming radiation.

Excessive exposure to those microwaves would warm, heat, burn your skin or hand, but not cause mutations in cells which could become malignant.

So, you won't be morphing into a microwave-induced superhero anytime soon. Still, let's not get too cozy. It's best to maintain a respectable distance, just in case your popcorn pops right out of the bag! Remember, it's the popcorn we need to watch out for, not the microwave.

Does sleeping with a heavy stomach give nightmares?

Actually it can. A heavy meal increases your metabolism which increases the activities in your brain. It increases your brainwaves and can cause nightmares.

Specially if you have a spicy dinner, sugary drinks or some particular medicines, you may end up having bad dreams.

A full stomach can also trigger acidity which may cause sleep disruptions and nightmares.

Can I fart my guts out accidentally?

Yes, you can, although it is highly unlikely. But this has happened to some people.

If you push too hard, you can actually roll the rectum in the wrong direction. You rectum and guts may get displaced from normal position and get pushed out of the anal opening. This is called "rectal prolapse".

So, don't push too hard when you fart or poop. That might send your intestines on a solo mission to the moon!

Can cracking your knuckles cause harm or lead to arthritis?

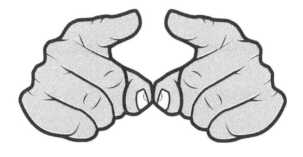

No, it doesn't.

When you crack them, you're basically letting out a tiny burst of gas that's been trapped in the joint, like a fizzy soda escaping its bottle. It's a bit like a minicelebration for your fingers!

Studies have shown that it's generally harmless. It won't lead to arthritis or any major joint issues. So, you can keep on popping those party favors without much worry!

However, a word of caution for the enthusiastic crackers among us: if it starts to hurt or feels uncomfortable, it might be a good idea to give your joints a little break.

Cracking knuckles may have some social consequences, depending on how often and how loudly you do it. If you crack your knuckles too much or too loudly, you may annoy or offend the people around you. You may even get into trouble with your boss or your teacher if you crack your knuckles during a meeting or a class.

So, if you do crack your knuckles, do it discreetly and respectfully.

How Can I Build a Nice Butt?

Oh, the quest for a amazing derrière! Having well-built glutes has many benefits: aesthetics, overall stability, strength, great posture and power.

Here are some smart workouts to get a bigger butt:

Squats, the Glute Grandmasters:

Imagine your glutes as two valiant knights, ready to conquer any hill. Squats are their training ground, where they bulk up and prepare for battle.

Lunges, the Stride of the Glute Warriors:

Picture your glutes striding boldly into battle. Lunges are their sword and shield, sculpting them into formidable assets.

Hip Thrusts, the Royal Rump Raiser:

Envision your glutes ascending a throne, ruling with majesty. Hip thrusts are their coronation ceremony, bestowing them with regal volume.

Deadlifts, the Glute Gladiator Challenge:

See your glutes donning armor and lifting

mighty weights. Deadlifts forge them into warriors, ready to face any booty battle.

Donkey Kicks, the Cheeky Charge:

Imagine your glutes as sprightly steeds, kicking with vigor. Donkey kicks train them to deliver powerful, perky kicks.

Booty Bridges, the Glute Gateway to the Stars:

Picture your glutes reaching for the celestial skies. Booty bridges are their cosmic catapult, launching them toward booty stardom.

The Treadmill Trek, the Glute Expedition:

Visualize your glutes embarking on an epic treadmill journey. Incline walking challenges them, sculpting them into finely tuned glute-adventurers.

Spectacular, isn't it?

When you notice that your trousers are tighter in your butt area, your thighs are changing, your waist looks smaller and you feel stronger, you're on to something.

Remember, consistency is the loyal squire in this quest. Feed your glutes with a balanced diet and plenty of water to keep them strong and hydrated. And a let your sense of humor be your trusty companion, for even in the pursuit of a "nice butt," laughter is the truest treasure!

Why Do Doctors Frequently Feel Testicles During Regular Visits?

Well, having someone touch your private parts can make you feel awkward and embarrassed, especially if you're not used to it. But don't worry, doctors are professionals who have seen and examined many testicles in their careers. They are not judging you or trying to make you uncomfortable. They are just doing their job, which is to keep you healthy.

By feeling the testicles and the area around them, doctors can detect any changes in size, shape, or consistency that might indicate a problem. Testicles are like nature's little beanbags of potential problems. They can occasionally harbor issues that, if caught early, are much easier to address. So, the doctor's gentle prodding and poking is their way of ensuring everything feels shipshape.

Can sex with a virgin cure you of AIDS?

That's a big, resounding NO.

Virgin cleansing myth is a dangerous and harmful myth that has no scientific basis whatsoever. In fact, having sex with a virgin can only increase the risk of transmitting HIV to another person.

AIDS is caused by the HIV virus. There is no cure for AIDS, but there are treatments that can help people live longer and healthier lives.

So, while romantic comedies might have you believe in the power of love, it's best to rely on science and medical professionals for HIV treatment. Safe practices and regular check-ups are the way to go!

The only virgin that can cure anything is extra virgin olive oil!

One of my testicles hangs lower than the other. Should I be worried?

It is completely normal.

Having one testicle hang lower than the other is normal. This happen because usually one testicle is a bit larger than the other. Since the larger testicle is heavier, it hangs a bit lower.

It's like nature's way of giving them some personal space. Having them on the same level would cause them rubbing against each other more. Having them in different level reduces this scenario.

Unless you notice any sudden changes or discomfort, consider it a quirk of your biology, not a cause for concern. Carry on with confidence!

Why does it feel so good to put a Q-tip in my ear?

The ear-cleaning bliss! Putting a Q-tip in your ear feels oddly satisfying, It's like giving your ear canal a mini massage. Those delicate nerve endings get a gentle tickle, and it's as if they're saying, "Thank you!" It's the closest thing to a spa day for your ears.

While it's a joyous endeavor, remember not to go all spelunking in there. The ear canal has its limits.

With a Q-tip, you can accidentally cause an eardrum rupture. It can cause severe pain and permanent damage to the ear drum.

Just be sure to keep it gentle and avoid going too deep – no need to turn it into an extreme sport.

Happy ear pampering!

What will happen if I hold my pee too long?

Holding in your pee for too long can lead to a comical dance of discomfort, as your bladder performs its own version of the Macarena.

It can lead to some unwelcome consequences. Your bladder can only hold so much before it starts sending urgent messages. Ignoring these signals can result in discomfort, potential urinary tract infections, or, in extreme cases, even kidney problems. There will be a buildup of excess electrolytes and cause harm.

So, while it might seem like a heroic feat to hold it in, it's better to find a restroom and give your bladder the release it deserves!

Why is my poop glowing green?

Don't worry. You are not turning into a green goblin. Here is a complementary question. Is the green goblin's crap green?

Anyways, may be because you had too much green, leafy vegetables. Bright green plants have lots of chlorophyll. It may cause the green color in your turd.

Certain antibiotics can cause a change in the types of bacteria present in your gut. This might cause green poop.

Excess bile in poop can cause this, too. Diarrheal conditions can cause food to move too quickly through your intestine. Hence, the bile pigment cannot break down properly resulting in green poop.

Norovirus and some other types of parasites can cause your gut to work faster than normal. This can impact stool color.

Why is the vein on my penis black? Is it normal?

If you've suddenly got a "rockstar" vein on your member, don't worry, it's not auditioning for a heavy metal band! Sometimes, blood vessels can appear more prominent due to increased blood flow or other factors.

The penile vein is just under the skin of your dick. Dark red blood flows through it, unlike the bright red blood that flows through the arteries. Because the vein is just under the skin, the color of the skin, the way light hits it, how much oxygen is in the blood and other factors might make it appear dark blue or even black. So, it is normal to have darkened veins.

But remember, if it's causing you concern, go to a doctor who can provide a professional explanation!

Can I store my tears in a jar and drink it?

Well, technically, tears are like the body's homemade, organic, gluten-free saline solution. But unless you're auditioning for a tear-jerking drama or planning an avant-garde cooking show, it's best to stick with regular water.

Unless you are suffering from conjunctivitis, your tears should be toxin-free. But bacteria may get mixed with the tears from the surface of the skin. When you keep the tears in a jar, those bacteria may grow with time. Then it may become dangerous to drink it.

Don't drink tears... please.

Is the color of a butthole dark naturally or does it become darker?

Naturally, the color of a butthole tends to be on the darker side due to the melanin pigmentation in the surrounding skin. It's like Mother Nature's way of saying, "This is where the sun don't shine!"

Some factors like age, genetics, and sun exposure can play a role. The color of the butthole can also change over time due to hormonal changes, friction, and inflammation. Friction from sex, clothing, or hygiene products can also cause inflammation, which can lead to darkening of the skin.

Now don't start a "Butthole Brightening" trend. It's perfectly normal for it to have its own unique hue.

How can I get rid of a boner quickly ?

Just enjoy it while you still got it, my friend!

Well, here are a few nifty tricks you can try to get rid of a boner asap:

The Sneaky Tuck and Roll: Find a private spot, and subtly tuck your friend into your waistband. Then, give a gentle, nonchalant roll to ensure everything's in its proper place. Voilà!

The Mental Distraction Technique: Engage your brainpower! Start thinking about the most mundane, non-sexy things you can conjure. Try mentally reciting the ingredients of your favorite breakfast cereal or composing a mental grocery list. Works like a charm!

The Sudden Exercise Regimen: Quickly

stand up and pretend you've just decided to do a series of impromptu squats. Your body will redistribute the blood flow, giving your over-eager friend something else to think about.

The Cold Shower Gambit: If you're near a bathroom, a cheeky splash of cold water on the nether regions can do wonders to cool the engines.

The Pocket Change Routine: Excuse yourself, as if you've just remembered you have a pressing matter in your pocket. Then proceed to subtly adjust and redirect the energy elsewhere.

The Masterful Concealment: Fashion a makeshift shield out of a conveniently placed book, laptop, or even a potted plant. This diversionary tactic will give you the cover you need to discreetly handle the situation.

Remember, humor and a light-hearted approach can be your best allies in these moments. Just relax, take a deep breath, and know that we've all been there. With a little creativity and a dash of wit, you'll master the art of boner vanquishing in no time!

Can I get blue balls?

Blue balls is a term that refers to the discomfort some individuals may experience when sexual arousal is not followed by release

It's like a traffic jam on the highway to pleasure-town, causing a bit of congestion in the nether regions.

When a person gets all hot, the blood vessels in the genital area swell with anticipation, gearing up for some action. If said action doesn't occur, the extra blood can cause a feeling of heaviness, tenderness, or, metaphorically speaking, a slight shade of blue in the testicles.

Now, let's address the burning question: Can you actually get blue balls? Absolutely! It's a real physical sensation for some folks, though the intensity and duration vary from person to person. It's not a medical emergency, mind you, just a temporary inconvenience.

The solution? Well, the obvious one involves finding a way to release the built-up tension. But fear not, if the stars don't align for you, a bit of time, a cold compress, or even a brisk walk can help ease the discomfort.

Remember, it's a natural occurrence, and there's no need to don a detective's hat or reach for a literal paint sampler to confirm its existence. Keep things flowing smoothly, and you'll steer clear of blue balls.

If I pull my dick too much, will I get cancer?

There is no direct link between masturbation

and cancer. Engaging in solo adventures in the privacy of your own company is perfectly normal and, dare I say, even healthy! It's like giving yourself a little spa day for your more intimate bits.

Now, it's essential to remember that like all good things in life, balance is key. If one were to embark on an Olympic-level training regimen of self-love, it might lead to some temporary soreness or chafing. But fear not, a little moderation and perhaps some quality lubrication can do wonders.

In fact, some studies even suggest that regular sexual activity, whether solo or with a partner, may have potential health benefits. It can help reduce stress, improve sleep, and boost your overall mood.

So, in a sense, you could say a healthy dose of self-love might just be a preventive measure against a bad case of the blues!

Why do I poop so much when I'm hung over?

When you indulge in a night of alcohol intake, your body can end up feeling a bit miffed at you. Alcohol is a diuretic, which means it encourages your kidneys to produce more urine. This leads to dehydration, and your body does its best to compensate by pulling water from wherever it can, including your intestines. Now, that extra water in your intestines can lead to rapid movements inside.. Your digestive system might decide to speed things up and empty out the pronto. So, you find yourself starring in your very own sequel to "Gone with the Wind."

Alcohol can also irritate the lining of your stomach and intestines, which can lead to cramping and an urgent need to expel the excess. When your liver gets to work breaking down the booze, it produces substances that can further irritate your gut, contributing to the urge for a speedy bathroom visit.

How can you prevent or treat this problem? Well, the best way is to drink less alcohol or avoid it altogether. But if you do drink, make sure to stay hydrated by drinking plenty of water. Eat some bland and nourishing foods, and treat your body with a little extra TLC after a night on the town.

Can a fart kill a person?

Highly unlikely. But in some seriously messed up circumstances, it can!

Farts are mostly composed of harmless gases like nitrogen, hydrogen, carbon dioxide, and methane. These gases are not toxic, but they can displace oxygen in a closed space, which can lead to asphyxiation. However, you would need a lot of farts to fill up a room with enough gas to suffocate someone. According to one estimate, it would take about 70,000 farts to kill a person in an average-sized room. That's a lot of farts!

Another way farts can be dangerous is if they are flammable. Methane and hydrogen are both combustible gases, and they can ignite if there is a source of fire nearby. This can cause burns, explosions, or even fires. But unless you are farting near a candle or a lighter, you are probably safe.

If you don't released the fart, you may develop lots of gas in the abdomen. In extreme cases, your abdomen may stretch out so much that it causes a bowel obstruction and even a bowl rupture. Then you may develop a serious health condition and potentially die.

However, your average everyday fart is about as threatening as a butterfly in a tutu. It might cause a giggle or a grimace, but it's not going to send anyone to the great beyond.

Does Masturbation Cause Hair Loss?

No, masturbation does not cause hair loss. Unless you are doing it so much that you are literally draining your body of vital nutrients, or pulling your hair out in excitement you have nothing to worry about.

Some people may think that masturbation causes hair loss because they believe that semen contains a lot of protein, and that losing protein through ejaculation can affect hair growth. However, this is not true.

Another myth is that masturbation increases testosterone levels, which in turn increases the levels of a hormone called DHT (dihydrotestosterone) that is linked to hair loss. However, there is no evidence that masturbation affects testosterone or DHT levels in any significant way.

The bottom line is that masturbation and hair loss are not related. There are many other factors that can influence your hair health, such as genetics, stress, nutrition, medication, and medical conditions.

Your hair follicles are unaware of your solo pleasure episodes, and they're not about to start a protest over it by falling off.

My dick bends when I get a boner. Is it normal?

This situation is often referred to as "penile curvature," Usually its nothing to worry about. In fact, it's perfectly normal for a penis to have a bit of a bend.

Now, there's a fancy term for more

pronounced bending: Peyronie's disease. It happens when scar tissue forms inside the penis, causing it to curve. If you suspect your shaft is bent too much, it might be a good idea to chat with a healthcare professional, just to make sure everything's in tip-top shape.

The thing is as long as you're not experiencing pain or discomfort, and your performance isn't impacted, there's probably no need to stress about it. Embrace your beautifully unique anatomy, my friend! After all, it's the quirks that make us interesting.

I hope you enjoyed this book. That's it for now! Take care.

Milton Keynes UK
Ingram Content Group UK Ltd.
UKHW011045231123
433129UK00005B/407